Shattered Image

Shattered Image

The Gift of Being Naked Before Friends

By Sherri Jefferson

ISBN-13: 978-0965465625
ISBN-10: 0965465624

This is a work of fiction. Names, characters, places, and incidents either are the product of the author's imagination or are used fictitiously. Any resemblance to actual persons living or dead, events, or locales is entirely coincidental.

Published and printed in the United States of America

Understanding the difference between character flaws and a flawed character is necessary. Lest we live in hell while waiting to get to a place called Heaven, let us learn to embrace and enjoy the true meaning of love and friendship.

"They that wait on the Lord shall renew their strength; they shall mount up with wings as eagles; they shall run and not be weary; they shall walk and not faint." Isaiah 40:31.

One

HOW WILL YOU REACT
WHEN TRAGEDY STRIKES

Snuggled in her chaise lounge, dressed in a flannel two-piece night set, and wearing thick white socks, Kenya braces for a cold New York night at home. She finally takes a moment out of her hectic schedule to call Ebony, who is one of her best friends. She and Ebony reminisce on their childhood days growing up in the city. As they shared their childhood memories, Ebony received an incoming call from Mahogany. She is calling to let Kenya know that their girlfriend Sahara is in the hospital in Atlanta. Mahogany wants everyone to fly to Atlanta to be there for Sahara and her five-year-old daughter, Diamond. Anxiously, Ebony said, "Girl, what is going on, what has happened?" Mahogany replies that her name was listed as next of kin and that the hospital did not give a lot of details, only that Sahara's family and friends need to be at the hospital.

Now frustrated by the circumstances, Ebony said, "See, I told you all that Sahara's day as a jump off were going to catch up with her." Cautiously, Mahogany replied, "We do not have time for name calling, Ebony, are you coming?" "Yes, Mahogany, but I am keeping it real, I am not saying nothing that I have not said in her face. Nevertheless, I will tell Kenya what is going on, she is on the other line." Ebony asked Mahogany, "Did you call Sahara's family?" Feeling overwhelmed, Mahogany said, "We are her family. Do you know someone else? Tell me something!" Emotionally distraught, Ebony clicked back to speak with Kenya, but before she could say anything, disappointed, Kenya screamed at Ebony for failing to return to the telephone sooner and for what she thought was disrespectful --- keeping her on hold. "Girl, the least you could do is come back to the line. I have other things that I could be doing than holding on the line!" Ebony said, "Listen, Kenya, that was Mahogany, Sahara is in the hospital in Atlanta and we all need to be there for her." "Oh! I am sorry! Well, what is wrong?" "I do not know exactly, but you know your girl, so there is no telling." Kenya asked Ebony, "Will you fly out tonight, and where are you staying?" Ebony responded, "We are all staying in Buckhead at a hotel near the mall." Kenya said that she did not have it like that and had other responsibilities.

Ebony told her that she will take care of everyone and that she just needed Kenya to make the reservations with the airline and hotel. "We need to fly out tonight and meet each other at the airport in Atlanta." Kenya said, "Let us just stay at Sahara's place." "What! Are you crazy! Heck no! No!" Ebony refused, saying, "Please, until I find out what is going on with Sahara, I am not sleeping in her bed or anywhere in her house. I will not use her utensils, towels, or nothing else." "You are crazy, Ebony." "No, I am not crazy. Kenya, we do not know what is wrong with her, so I'd rather stay at the hotel, thank you very much!" Irate, Ebony said, "Am I the only one who can see? Am I the only one who knows that Sahara is out there? Surely, you are not telling me that the thought has not crossed your mind that she has AIDS." "Well, I am not prejudging anybody, but I will make reservations and call you back, Kenya, so please check on Mahogany."

Two

TO JUDGE OR NOT TO JUDGE

Ebony, Mahogany, and Kenya all arrived at the airport in Atlanta. Before checking into the hotel, they decided to go directly to the hospital before visitation ended. Sahara was in the intensive care unit (ICU). Mahogany went to the nurses' station to inquire about Sahara's condition. The nurse advised her to wait and discuss Sahara's condition with her physician. Mahogany also asked about Sahara's daughter, Diamond. The nurse said that the schoolteacher, Ms. Hopkins, took the child to stay with her. Mahogany requested the phone number and called Ms. Hopkins to speak to Diamond.

As the three waited nervously to get permission to visit with Sahara, Mahogany led them in prayer. She recited Psalm 101 and Deuteronomy 7:9, and when she concluded Ebony exclaimed, "Mahogany, I know that you were talking about me when you recited Psalm 101. However, I am not prejudging Sahara or speaking ill will toward her. I am merely saying that no matter what I have told her over the years about being with different men, she refused to listen, and it is like talking to a brick wall. I would rather speak my mind openly, than to think it and not share it." Mahogany said, "Ebony, who are you to judge? The Bible says in John 7:24 that we should 'stop judging by mere appearance, and make a right judgment.'"

Pissed off, Ebony replied, "Look, it is late, and I did not come down here for a sermon, and I know the Bible, too. I know if I subject myself to judgment, then I can judge other people. Miss Evangelist, I suggest that you read Luke 6:37 and Matthew 7:1, and then go preach on the street corner. Further, while you are doing that, read John 8:16, because it says, 'but if I do judge, my decisions are right, because I am not alone. I stand with the Father who sent me.'"

"Ebony, who said he sent you?" declared Mahogany. Then Ebony responded, "The God that sent me is the same God that told you that you were an evangelist. Mahogany replied, "Yeah, right! I do not think so. You are not the only person who knows God, Mahogany; holy rollers kill me thinking you are the only people who know God and His Word. You are judging me right now because you assume that since I do not attend church the way you do and openly express my faith or belief in God that I do not know God." Apologetic, Mahogany said, "That is not true, Ebony." "Yes, it is, yes, it is!" "Whatever! I am going to see Sahara," Ebony exclaimed. "I did not come to Atlanta for this drama." Mahogany told Ebony to wait. However, Ebony refused to do so, saying, "No, Miss Evangelist, you have to wait. I did not come here to be in the waiting room, I came to be by her side, remember!"

Kenya agreed and along with Ebony walked into Sahara's room. Frail with an appearance of severe weight loss, Sahara had an IV and was on life support, she was unconscious. Shortly after they entered the room, the doctor and the nurse arrived. The doctor said that it was okay for all of them to be in the room, they briefly discussed that they were pleased that the family had come to visit with her. Ebony asked if Sahara could have her own room, but the nurse said that she understood Sahara to be uninsured. Ebony volunteered to pay the cost to move her to a private room, but the nurse told her to consult with the admissions and billing department. Ebony went to the billing department, and while in the billing department, a representative explained that even though Sahara was uninsured, it did not affect the level of care she would be entitled to receive. The representative opposed Ebony's offer to pay for a private room, because she said that at this stage Sahara would not be aware of her surroundings anyway.

Ebony disagreed and said, "There is a difference between the level of care that she is entitled to and what she will actually receive." Ebony begged to differ and shared her personal childhood experience with the representative based upon an inaccurate diagnosis of a childhood mental and behavioral disorder. Ebony explained briefly how as a child the children teased her because of her enrollment in special education classes. She told the billing clerk that her parents did not have private insurance to address her disorder. They had Medicaid coverage. She explained that because she only had Medicaid, she did not receive quality health care and that her parents' options were very limited. She recalled how easy it would have been, in hindsight, for her to receive counseling for child abuse, but due to her insurance status, services were not available in her community. Ebony told the representative that her parents were the working poor. She concluded by saying that is why she attained her M.B.A. and a Ph.D. She said that as a corporate executive and business owner, she wants to help Sahara.

The representative explained that ICU did not generally place patients in private rooms, regardless of their income or status. She admired Ebony's stance and assured her that the best thing she could do for Sahara was to use her money for aftercare services and treatment. Further, that as long as her friends were at the hospital every day and visibly inquiring about Sahara's condition and treatment, she would get the best care possible. Ebony thanked her for her assistance. Ironic, during this dialogue they never discussed Sahara's diagnosis or the aftercare.

Upon returning to the room, Ebony noticed that Mahogany was on the telephone with Diamond. Diamond was so excited to hear from her mommy's friends, she called them her aunties. Mahogany asked Ms. Hopkins if she could pick Diamond up and take her to eat and talk for a while. Ms. Hopkins agreed and thought that familiarity would be great for Diamond during this time. Visitation was over at 8 p.m., and Mahogany did not want to keep Diamond out late, and she did not want to leave Sahara. Therefore, they agreed to bring Diamond to the hospital and eat in the cafeteria so that they would not leave Sahara. In addition, Diamond could at least know her mommy's whereabouts. Diamond could not see her mommy because she was in ICU. They were all together in the cafeteria talking and laughing, and no one asked Diamond about what happened to her mother.

Three

DYING TO THE FLESH,
THE POWER OF SELF-REVELATION

Later that evening, they checked into the hotel. They reserved a suite to accommodate all of them. Mahogany was the first to awake. She awoke at 3 a.m. and engaged in prayer, praise, and worship. She did not disturb anyone, she went into the bathroom and put on her headphones and played her iPod. She cried out to the Lord, and she interceded for Sahara. During her quiet time with the Lord, she reflected on His goodness, grace, and mercy. She reflected on how she always envied Sahara's beauty, her tall, slender build, long hair and her light complexion. Equally so, she reflected on how much she used to hate herself for being dark-skinned and fat with short hair. She set a goal of trying to live by society's definition of beauty.

Throughout her life, she dieted and wore a wig or hair weave in order to fit into Madison Avenue and Hollywood's image of beauty, never realizing that an overwhelming majority of the women in this country will not fit that image and never will. In fact, other people always told her that no man would ever want her based on how she looked. Therefore, she suffered mental and emotional abuse, this abuse transcended into physical abuse as she began abusing her body by dieting, using drugs and alcohol, as well as engaging in sexual promiscuity.

During Mahogany's prayer, God really ministered to her needs and addressed her self-esteem issues. He also revealed to her how with His help she overcame the desire to commit suicide. Leading up to that, He continuously revealed to her that the pictures in the magazine and television were just that, mere images. As there is no singular truth in those images, as the truth was different for every woman. God revealed to her that it was deceptive advertisement because it did not reflect reality; its goal was to change reality, to distort the reality of millions of girls and women who are not a size 4 or smaller. The American fitness craze is intended to force people to fit a specific definition of beauty. So many girls have bought into the image by spending millions of dollars having surgery, going to the health spas, and attending fitness centers, as well as going on diets and paying for food and various services to "fit" the image. For girls like Mahogany, the image was unattainable. Thus, she envied Sahara for having the perfect image, and she hated herself for not being perfect. In the process, she forgot about the wonderful qualities that God gave her, like her inner and outer beauty, her intelligence, compassion, wittiness, ability to be domesticated, moreover, her love for people in need.

While crying out to the Lord, Mahogany remembered running away from New York, where she thought life was harsh. She moved to Tennessee. She soon learned that regardless of living in the perfect environment that people were cruel, and life was cruel. She learned that although created in God's image that God did not create her self-image. She realized until she lived for God that she will remain in bondage. This is true, no matter where she lived, no matter her education or employment status. God is graceful and merciful; He revealed to her that her characteristics were the same as some of the most prominent women in the world. God has blessed women who come in all shapes, sizes and skin tones, including women of brown and ebony skin hues.

These women include, but are not limited to, Queens of Africa to the Queen of Talk Show. God has blessed these women to be intellectual scholars, as well as divas of music and the arts. Women of brown and ebony hue serve as members of Congress, the first woman to run for President of the United States, as well as the First Lady of the United States. These women also include all of the Freedom Fighters and Abolitionists who led the way to freeing people from slavery. God gave Mahogany the tools to free herself from mental and emotional bondage. He taught her that all of these women in our history are either full figured and/or of brown and ebony skin tone. She realized that while society considers most African-American women of a lighter skin tone to be "beautiful," some of the most powerful women of our time are the brown or ebony hue. God allowed Mahogany to take her pick between being powerful and a world changer, or just beautiful? He taught her that she could have it all!

By the time she concluded her prayer, Kenya awoke to use the restroom. Kenya appeared to be perplexed, but said nothing. Later, they all departed to visit with Sahara at the hospital. Kenya asked Mahogany to do a group prayer in the room. So they all prayed, after praying Kenya wanted to comb Sahara's hair and bathe her. She asked if they could have a clean gown. The nurse said they have nursing assistants trained to fulfill her request. Kenya responded in the negative by saying that she was a trained, certified, and employed R.N. with a Master of Science in Nursing Degree and more than qualified to change the nightgown of her sister/friend! Furthermore, she added that Sahara had smelled very bad and that her hair was matted. The nurse obliged her request and told a CNA (Certified Nurse Assistant) to get Kenya a gown and basin for washing and to change her bed linen.

Kenya combed Sahara's hair and bathed her. After the linen was changed, they all sat in the room talking as though

Sahara could talk back to them or with them. Kenya and Ebony picked up from where they left off on the telephone, they started reminiscing again. Kenya then spoke about how she met Sahara in a foster home in Queens, NY. How they were close from day one, she spoke about how they were four years old and scared to death to live amongst strangers in the group home environment.

Ebony interjected by saying, "I never knew that the both of you were in foster care." She wanted Kenya to explain her foster care experience. "Why were you in foster care, you have a lot of family in New York?" Lyric and loud, Kenya said, "I told you that I was in foster care years ago!" "I do not recall hearing this story." Kenya did not understand what information Ebony needed to know. She replied, "I want to know what foster care was like for you." "Well, for Sahara and I, or based on my personal experience?" "Whichever, I just want to know your foster care experience," Ebony replied. "Come to think of it," Mahogany said, "after all of these years, I do not recall you speaking of foster care. I thought your life was better than mine. After all, Kenya, you took care of both of your parents. In fact, you take care of your mother now."

Kenya responded, "Well, like I was saying, we were only four and both scared to death of living amongst strangers. Uh, my father was on drugs very bad. Um, first the heroin, then crack cocaine. He went from selling to using, and you know you cannot survive using your own supply! My mom was in her 30s when my father got sick, he was very sick, but no one told me what was wrong. I know his organs malfunctioned. He had a heart and a liver condition. I watched how the nurses cared for him; I observed how the hospital and doctors treated him as an uninsured African-American man with a history of drug and alcohol abuse. In fact, that was the driving force that made me become a nurse. He was always in and out of the hospital." Ebony said, "We remember that your father was in the hospital a lot. Nevertheless, why were you in foster care?" "Actually, you do not remember all of it; you only recall my life when I was in high school, Ebony."

"My first encounter with foster care was because my father was using drugs, and we did not have food, clothing, or a place to live. The caseworker took me to Queens to live in a group home. I was only four years old. That is when I met Sahara and we became best friends. We remained in placement for two years and went to school together. I went back to live with my mother when I was six years old." Ebony said, "Wait a minute, where was your mother when you were in placement?" Kenya replied, "She lived from one place to the other. My father's family is in New York, but my mother was not from N.Y. She did not know anybody, and she was young. My father took good care of us until he started using drugs. He has a degree in Engineering, you know. My father is not a B.U.M. - he is not a Black Unemployed/Uneducated/Unsuccessful/Unaccomplished Male - he was smart, but the drugs really consumed him. Then, my mother started drinking. The displacement started after this ordeal."

Nested in her chair with her legs crossed and holding a cup of tea, Kenya continued sharing her story and said, "The problem that I have with the system is that they never helped and they did not provide my mother with the resources and tools needed to get back on her feet. These tools would have allowed her to survive on her own without my father. My father went into a treatment program through his job. My father's family did not help him or us. However, when the money was coming in from work and dealing, they were there with their hands out. He put his brother and sister through college. He helped them with their children. No one came to help my mother. Child Protective Services did not ever call his family, but my mother called them to no avail."

Ebony blatantly asked Kenya how she became separated from her siblings and allowed to live in a foster care home instead of living with relatives. Kenya replied, "Contrary to what CPS tells people, they do not notify the next of kin, family, or friends of the family." Angrily, Kenya said, "In fact, a family friend offered to keep me, but CPS said no. My mother told me that the family friend went to them to try to help." Eager to understand Kenya's plight, Mahogany asked, "Did your mother try to contact any of her family to help you so that you would not have to go into a foster home?" Ebony had many questions as well, because she just could not understand how the system allowed a little girl to go and live in a foster care home with strangers instead of helping her mother to become self-sufficient.

Frustrated by Ebony's actions and judgmental personality, Kenya said, "You know, Ebony, you are always judging; you have something to say for everything." She took offense to Ebony's questions and expressed her hurt. She said, "That is why I really do not like sharing with you." "Well, get over it," Ebony replied. "The fact is, people prefer to live in excuses, denial and justification rather than live in truth." Unapologetic, Ebony said, "I am merely asking questions. You would rather blame the system and your father's side of the family than to question why your mother's side of the family did not help you. All of them are wrong, the system and your family!" Kenya said, "I was not making excuses, Ebony, I was explaining what happened to me, and you do not understand."

Four

I THOUGHT YOU KNEW

Ebony expressed that she understood foster care because of her personal experiences. She explained, "I lived in seven homes -- 4 group homes and three private homes. They treated me worse than my family could have ever treated me in a lifetime. They beat me all of the time. I suffered broken arms, fractured ribs, sprained ankles, missing teeth, and blackened eyes. All separate incidents. The system's answer was to move me to another placement, that is, when my bruises or injuries were visible. No one came to check on me, not the caseworker or my family. They said I was a special child, with special needs. They said I had mental and behavioral disorders." Laughing aloud, Kenya said, "And you do!"

Laughing, Ebony continued, "I fought every day at school, mostly because of fear and shame. I went to school bruised, but the school did not report my abuse. CPS reports came from the hospital. I went to school with dirty clothes, hand me downs, and my hair always needed combing. I felt horrible. During my period, I used toilet tissue. In fact, I do not recall any of the group homes or private homes giving me underarm deodorant or personal toiletries. Before foster care placement, my parents were working, but we were what the system called 'working poor people' or the working poor. Then my father left, just left us, and never came back. My mother is a soldier, and she held down the fort. She managed

21

two jobs, kept us clean, provided us with a very nice home, and we were doing great in school, all of us."

Standing in the corner of the room wearing knee high boots and a sweater dress, expressing her hurt and pain, Ebony said, "The system gave us nothing, but took everything that we had, CPS took our family. It was in December; she was working a double shift on her second job. The police arrived at our house with a caseworker, and she said someone reported that we were home alone and that our mother had been leaving us unattended." Crying, Ebony explains her journey through the foster care system. "The person or persons who reported it should have helped us. Instead, they destroyed us. I was 5 years old, my brother was 8 years old, and my sister was eleven years old. They said she was too young to care over us while my mother was at work. They told us that the placement was going to be temporary. We cried to be together, but the caseworker said they did not have anyone who would take siblings, especially a boy of my brother's age. CPS sent my brother and sister to separate group homes, and they sent me to a private home. The caseworker and police promised that we would all be together for court when my mother appeared. I did not know how to spell their names. My sister had a different last name than my brother and I. I searched for them for years, all to no avail."

Kenya wanted to know why Ebony asked her so many questions. "I just wanted to know your experience," she replied. "Well, where was your family?" Ebony smirked. "CPS notified my family, but they never came for us. I mean, we waited the first night, and they would not give us back to our mother. My mother worked so hard, she did everything for us." Crying, Ebony said, "Both the caseworker and police officer promised us that we would be able to go home with our mother. However, we never saw her again. A day became a year, and a year became a lifetime. I do not recall going to court to return home, but I do recall going to court when they moved me from group homes because of abuse. I watched the caseworkers and lawyers in the city with their suits on, and I saw how they treated African-American children who were in the system. The prejudice is two sides, it is racial and social, because children experience bias based upon their race and our own people show impartiality based on social status. That is, some who are affluent, both academically and financially, treat us worse than others do."

Ebony continues, "These children were oftentimes neglected by their own families, no one cared, and no one at all. I mean, how do you allow strangers to raise your own blood? How do you know that your loved ones suffer maltreatment or mistreatment and sit idle and do nothing to assist?" Ebony kept saying "how" repeatedly to herself. "So Kenya, it is not just about the system, African-Americans have as many children in foster care than any other race or ethnicity of people. African American children are more likely to be in foster care, but less likely adopted when placed in care because most foster parents only want the check. Extended family members do not participate in reunification plans or assist their beloved ones. Why does CPS/DHR allow foster parents to keep children for years with no intent to adopt? Anyway, I vowed to get my education, make money, and help as many children as possible. I went to college and graduate school, as well as worked and saved to start my business. That is why I am so committed to community outreach and am an activist for children. We look for everyone else to come into our communities and give. We have a duty, and no one owes us anything.

"We have neglected our future generations because we are waiting on the same system who takes our children and tears apart our families with no help toward reunification to turn around and give us something back. It is never going to happen! In the past as a people, we always took care of our own, but now we are self-centered and it is all about me, me, and me! I think it is wonderful to feed and give to needy causes overseas, but you do not have to go overseas or to another country to see poverty, famine, and disease. Right here, in parts of Atlanta, you can see it, and God only knows it is in New York. Look at Washington, D.C., it is a world with two sides, the rich and affluent and the poor and disenfranchised. Look further and examine South Central Los Angeles. Furthermore, consider places like Rural Georgia, the Delta of Mississippi, Rural Alabama, or New Orleans."

Sharing her thoughts, Ebony continues and expresses that New Orleans was like a third world country well before Hurricane Katrina. "The media just televised the area of Mardi Gras. People never saw the real New Orleans. Nothing is new about New Orleans, New York or New Jersey. These cities are in ruins, and they are plagued with drugs, crime, dilapidated buildings, and people incarcerated and undereducated. The inner city communities are plagued with a D.I.G. mentality of drugs, drunkenness, illiteracy, ignorance, guns and greed. Meanwhile, there exist spirits of liquor and church filled houses on every corner, but this is not the vehicle out of poverty, addiction and criminality. We must decide between education and incarceration. We must decide between poverty, sickness and disease or education, employment and healthcare."

Unstoppable, Ebony continues claiming that agencies defrauded the victims of Katrina. She asks, "Think about how the private organizations and small churches gave money to help Katrina victims before the mega churches? While the mega churches hit the airwaves begging for more money, I wanted to know what were they doing with the millions they already banked. To this day, the victims are scattered all over the country like refugees, it was like seeing a slave auction, you went wherever the agencies sent you, even without all of your children. Most African-Americans did not have family in neighboring areas where they could go and live.

"Women and children were all over the place, I was wondering, where are the men? All of these women with babies crying out for help, and no men in sight. We continue to cry foul that no men are around, well, where are the babies coming from if there are no men? All around this country, we continue to struggle. We have no one to blame but ourselves. We are wealthier now as a people than ever before, but are less likely to give. Our ancestors taught us to embrace the songs of yesteryear like begging to overcome or for freedom, but until we realize that freedom is a state of mind, we will always be behind." Mahogany said, "Girl, do not get Ebony started, because she will keep going!" Ebony said, "Well, it's crazy! Just to think, they said I had the mental and behavioral disorder!" Laughing, Kenya replied, "You do!"

"Girl, I almost forgot what we were talking about." Ebony continues, "Oh yeah! We were discussing my foster care experience, right? Anyway, my heart ached every day, I was a child who yearned for her mother's love and affection. I desired to be with family, my family, but I was empty. There is still a void in me that I am unable to fill. I think that is why I am single today with no children. It would drive me crazy if I had to experience attachment and then be subject to detachment again."

Speechless, Mahogany said, "Wow! Ebony, I am so sorry to hear this. All of these years, and I never made the connection. I thought that you were just career oriented." "Yeah, girl, that too," smiles Ebony, "because without an education and money, you are nothing in this world. Yes, nothing. You can claim God, profess your faith, but none of that matters as the churches are full of poor people struggling every day with issues like shelter, food, healthcare, and employment. If my mother were well educated and had money, they would have never taken us." "Well, Ebony, that is not quite true, you have Jesus and you have to believe in Him," said Mahogany. "Tell that to a child who is forced away from her mother and siblings," replied Ebony. Mahogany said, "Do not be mad at God, because but for this experience, hundreds of children would not be blessed by your generosity, you are the sacrificial lamb. In addition, now that you found your mother, you can renew your adult life with her and make a better life for her. You say that is why you moved to Texas, to be closer to your mother and to find your sister and brother. Right?"

Kenya wanted to know how Ebony knew of her family's whereabouts in Texas. Ebony replied, "I did not know, actually, a relative said they heard my mother went looking for us and she left New York for Texas. My brother supposedly was in prison in Texas for drug trafficking, according to this relative. She went there to find him. Therefore, I went there to find them." Kenya said, "What about your sister?" Ebony replied, "We do not know her location, but we have been given different leads, but nothing so far is legitimate. All right, enough about me, how did this become about me anyway?"

Ebony asked Kenya to finish telling her story, because she was so moved and shocked by her life story. Ebony said, "Just to think, I thought that I knew you. My image of you is shattered." Kenya told Ebony that she made her a goddess, because she said, "You are so strong, untouchable, and seem to have it all together." Kenya said, "Your life experiences are full of pain." "Well, Ebony, some people create an image based on low self-esteem, others based upon their socio-economic status, etc., but your very essence is from pain," Kenya said. She went on to say, "I do not want you to miss the joys of life. Life can still offer you marriage and children. Marriage and children can be great. You can also take care of your mother, just like me."

Five

WHILE SHE SLEPT

Ebony desired for Kenya to continue conveying her foster care experience. Disturbed by Ebony's demands for more answers, Kenya said, "Okay, Ebony, they sent me back to live with my family. My father was clean for a while. Everything was great! Then he got sick, and we had no income. My mother was one of those pretty girls with great looks, but no education. She aspired to marry a man with money. My father never thought about the future. If he did, he would have married someone who could provide for us in a time of need. Her beauty took her as far as it could go, so when my father took ill, there was no money saved, and we started going from place to place. We slept in the car, but visited with Daddy every day. Someone at the hospital realized that we were sleeping in our car, and bathing and changing at the hospital. They called Child Protective Services. Long and short, I was sent back to foster care. I was only nine years old. I did not see Sahara, but several months later she came to my school. I had gotten into a fight, the teacher sent me to the principal's office, and she was in the office." Ebony wanted to know why Sahara was in foster care, and Kenya said, "I do not know; you will have to ask her that when she awakes."

Finally, Kenya gets to continue to share her story. "Sahara and I clicked again." Mahogany said, "Wow, she was in foster care, too!" "Yeah, in fact, she was in there since she was four years old. Only this time, she was in another group home. I

27

was in private placement. One day, she ran away and came to my placement. I let her enter through the window. I told my foster mother that she was with us, and she called CPS. They said she could remain until they sent a caseworker. Well, the caseworker never came. Therefore, my foster mother went to the CPS office and spoke with them. I do not know everything they spoke about, because I was not there, but they took Sahara back to the group home. I cried so much, because she was dirty and you can tell that she was unkempt. I did not see Sahara in school for a long time. Then, during summer break, we both turned 10 years old, and the kids in the community were saying bad things about her, but I never saw her. A couple of months later, after school started, she was getting out of a car late at night. She was by herself, and my foster mother noticed an older person in the car. She got his license plate and screamed out to Sahara to come to us immediately. She was crying, she smelled so bad and her clothes were dirty. Her hair was unkempt and matted together. My foster mother called CPS and told them that Sahara was going to stay with us whether they helped us or not.

"The following day, she took Sahara to the doctor. I do not know the outcome, but she was taking medicine for a while. I loved Sahara as if she was my own sister. She is smart, and she was doing great in school, we did everything together for two years. Then, after my twelfth birthday, my family was able to get me back. I asked them to get Sahara, but they could not. Sahara was able to remain with our foster mother. Thereafter, my family moved, so I did not see or hear from Sahara until we were sophomores in high school." Mahogany interrupted and said, "By then, all of us were friends." "Yes," Kenya replied. Ebony said, "I did not know you and Sahara had so much history, interesting!"

Kenya said, "Oh well, you all know the story from there, and Sahara wanted the American Dream by then. Just like my mother. She ended up doing dance videos and modeling with some agency in Manhattan. After graduation, she moved in with an athlete in New Jersey. Actually, they did not live together, per se. He kept her by giving her a condominium, car, and money. When he finished with her, she met another athlete who moved her to Indiana. When that failed, she met a producer from New York, who moved her to Miami. Finally, when that failed, she was a complete jump off. Thereafter, she ended up with a drug dealer and stripping in a club here in Atlanta. Then she became pregnant with Diamond. The father either is in prison or is married, because she never talks about him. Some say that he is a professional athlete and he disowned his child."

Ebony interjected and said, "That is not always the case, maybe things just did not work out. Regardless, he should be an active participant in his child's life. Unless Sahara has denied him the chance to participate in Diamond's life, he has no excuse for not being an active father. Many mothers deny their children relationships with their fathers when they use the child as a pawn to get back at the father. One of the main reasons why so many children are in CPS/DFACS custody or in prison is because no father is in the home and there is no relationship with the paternal side of the family. Women are only hurting themselves and their children when they prevent fathers who want to be active in their child's life from doing so."

Ebony continues, "Furthermore, the relationship and child support is not about the mother, it is about the child. As women, we have to know when to let go and let God. Let the children have their relationship with their fathers. Men have to be willing to set aside their feelings and be there for their children. Men have to be more than sperm donors and seed planters; they must be an intricate part of their children's lives. Our communities are full of single parent households, some by choice, most by default. Uncle Sam and Aunt

Samantha are not responsible for rearing our children. Almost 500,000 children are in the foster care system, the majority are children of color. More than 1.9 million men and women are in prison, the majority are men and women of color. Parenting is a full-time job, and we never retire from it. We have to learn to be better parents and better human beings. For the sake of our children and the future of society, we have to make things right. To do so means to be more responsible, more accountable and more accessible. We have a President of African origin, and we are still singing and writing songs that invoke sex, drugs and violence. Our songs disrespect women and misinterpret love and sex. We are no better off than we were before the 2008 election." Kenya said, "Man, Ebony, all of this from a simple statement about Diamond's father."

"Sixty-seven percent of our households are female headed, some by choice and others by default. It is bigger than Diamond's father." Ebony explained that the root of our problem is self and no one else. "We cannot continue to live in excuses, denial and justification. Surely, racism is real, sexism is real, but complacency is also real." "I still do not know why all of this is important, Ebony, because God knows what he is doing." "Ebony said, "You are right, Mahogany, and He wants us to know what we are doing, too. We cannot continue to hide behind religion, tradition and spirituality.

"Furthermore, everything that I said is important in understanding why Sahara went to foster care. It is important," Ebony exclaimed, "because a close family member sexually abused Sahara as a child, and that is why she was in foster care. Then, while in CPS custody, the abuse continued and no one watched over her. She suffered at the hands of the community, and no one came to her rescue. The point that I was trying to make is that we just do not care anymore."

Frustrated, Kenya said, "Okay, Ebony, your point is well taken, now let me continue. Anyway, one night we saw Sahara with some man, he was not related to her and he was not with CPS either. Therefore, Ebony, you are wrong to prejudge Sahara as being a person without morals and values." "Wait a minute! I never accused Sahara of lacking morals or values," Ebony replied. Kenya said, "No, not now, but you have in the past." "Sahara has felt dirty and ugly her entire life, and she strips off her grave clothes, all of her fears, shame, guilt, and hurt. Well, she wanted the American Dream, and she soon realized that the dream was a nightmare," Ebony replied, "and we all make choices, me included. She graduated from school just like us, she chose a different route, and there is nothing wrong with that, except there are consequences." Kenya said that Sahara did not have any family. "Her mother's side of the family beats her, and the men sexually abused her and called her names. Her father's side of the family remains unknown. She has been in CPS custody since she was four years old. Her mother is white, and her father supposedly is African-American." Ebony said, "Okay, we know that she is bi-racial!" "No, she is African-American, Ebony." "No. She is bi-racial. I am African-American, I passed through the womb of an African-American woman, and my father is an African-American. She cannot have it both ways." "Well, society considers her African-American." "Well, I am society, and I consider her bi-racial! The very notion that a person of bi-racial origin can claim to be only one race or in this circumstance, African-American, comes from a racist premise. The premise is a form of superiority wherein one race precludes the other from the right to claim their heritage or lineage." Ebony continued and said, "The bottom line is, Sahara looks as white as she does African-American, but society does not consider her white. Why?

"The theory behind this premise is that a drop of any other blood than white is not pure. Which, by its sure implication, proposes that the person of mixed race is inferior to the pure race. African Americans have bought into this foolishness by playing the numbers game, the Census Bureau numbers. The same way some of the Latin community has bought into this notion that Puerto Rican, Dominican, Cuban and Mexican is an actual race of people. Hispanic is not a race. Hispanic includes African and European origin. Hispanic is a group of ethnicities and nationalities. We divide our country between race, cultures, ethnicities, and nationalities. We keep people divided when we assert they must choose one or the other, and sadly most people do not want to be associated with African origin or Black, so it's easier to say I am Puerto Rican or Dominican, as opposed to Afro-Cuban or Afro-Dominican, etc. It is all so crazy how a few people make us decide who and what we are in life."

Kenya exclaimed, "ALL RIGHT! Ebony, you made your point!" "Well, if I have made my point, then accept the fact that Sahara is as white as she is black." Laughing, Ebony said, "Let us call her our Ivory Sista. Nevertheless, stop forcing me to say that she is African-American. She could also be a Tiger, because after all a tiger has two stripes!" Laughing aloud, the girls say, "Oh no, oh no, um, she is a zebra, and our brown and ebony mixes are tigers! Gotta have some humor." "All right, I understand what you are saying, but Sahara is still our girl," Kenya replied. "No doubt, I do not dispute that, but we do need an understanding about this race thing," said Ebony. "I am tired of people jumping in and out of our race when it is convenient for them based on this notion of what is or is not Black or African." Believing Ebony to be too harsh, Kenya said, "Sahara is not like that, and you know it." Ebony agreed. Kenya continued sharing Sahara's upbringing. "Anyway, as I was saying before you cut me off, Sahara remains disconnected from her heritage. She does not know how to love or how to care about men. She defines love as pain." Ebony responded, "No, Sahara equates love as material possessions or money, and that is not black or white, that is a choice that people make, it has nothing to do with race or ethnicity." Kenya agreed. "Sahara chose her life and her destination, and she has to give God the opportunity to channel her in the direction that He has destined her to be."

Six

MY HUSBAND SAYS HE HAS BEEN DELIVERED FROM HOMOSEXUALITY

Mahogany said, "You know, to change the subject a bit, it is ironic that I always envied her. I thought that I was ugly and fat." Laughing aloud, Ebony said, "You are! Okay, girl, I am just joking. Everything got so serious, so I was toning it down a bit." "As I was saying," Mahogany replied, "I thought that I was ugly and fat and always thought Sahara was so beautiful. Earlier today, I was talking to God about His goodness, grace, and mercy. I reflected upon my life. Funny, I did drugs, alcohol and engaged in sexual promiscuity. All trying to feel loved, I was full of shame, guilt, and pain. Gosh! Kenya, guess your life is better after all."

Kenya said, "How you figure, Mahogany?" "Well, you are married with two wonderful children, and you still take care of your mother since your father passed away." Kenya said, "Please, I wish life were that simple. I am grateful in all things, but I recently discovered that my husband has not been faithful." "What! You are kidding! He has a lot of nerve, as ugly as he is, he ought to be lucky that you even married him," said Ebony. "Heck, if he is cheating on you, he is not only unfaithful, but also ungrateful. He has a lot of nerve, as ugly as he is, he ought to be happy that you paid him any attention." Kenya exclaimed, "You do not know when to quit,

Ebony! Shut up, just shut up and listen." Mahogany said, "Ebony, personally speaking, I am sick of you, too. You are really showing your true colors today!" "I can show my true colors because I am amongst true friends. I cannot do this in Texas."

Kenya said, "Let me finish telling you all what happened. About 5 years ago, I was cleaning the attic, making room for some of my mother's belongings, when I came across his trunk from college." Ebony said, "Five years ago, how long is this story?" Kenya said, "Just shut up and listen! This is serious, Ebony. I prepared to throw away some of the composition books and his ruler bound books from old lectures when I came across some poems. The poems were love letters and signed only with initials. Therefore, I immediately went through his yearbooks, looking for a female with those initials. I never found her, so I shared the letters with my mother, and she said it is the past and let the past stay in the past.

"Two years ago, I found another letter expressing love for him, signed with the same initials. I asked him about it, and he said she was an old friend from college and that it was nothing. I prayed about it and tried to put it to rest. However, the issue remained unsettled in my soul and mind." Kenya continues by adding that the situation never left her mind and that she trusted God to work it all out. She recalled reading First Corinthians, Chapter 7 and thirteen about Godly love and relationships. However, several months later, an invitation arrived in the mail for his college reunion. "His fraternity brother called and asked if he would attend. I have known his fraternity brother only by his pledge name, but I gave my husband the message. We never discussed it further.

"Finally, months passed, and we arranged to attend the reunion. The date arrived, and we attended. Jokingly, I asked my sorority sister who is married to one of his fraternity brothers if she knew a female with those initials who went with her and my husband to school. She replied no but said that by the end of the evening, she would find out for me. At the close of the evening, she told me that by all accounts, those initials belonged to a man. She said no female had those initials that had gone to school with them. My mouth dropped. Afraid to inquire any further, I walked away. Moments later, she came over to me and pointed out the male with those initials. It was his fraternity brother. Yeah! The same dude who called the house to inquire if he would attend the reunion. Astonished, I immediately exited the building and asked the valet to bring my vehicle. I left word for him to come now or catch a ride back to the hotel. He came running toward me. I drove the car like a crazy woman who had escaped from the mental institution. I told him to shut his mouth and not to say a word! Finally, I demanded to check out the hotel and fly back to New York. He joined me. I did not exchange any words with him. Upon arrival, I checked on my mother and the children and then demanded to speak with him in private. In the course of communicating with him, I learned that he had a relationship with his fraternity brother during college. He said the relationship was sexual and ended in his senior year. He swore he had not had any other relationships, with either male or female, since we were married."

Ebony said, "You know that is not the point, because HIV/AIDS is rampant in our community and bad choices have to do with our plight, bad choices that we make as women to engage in unprotected sex, and the other is because of men on the D.L. and their decision to be less than honest. We owe it to ourselves to be proactive in protecting our bodies from sickness and disease. The fasting growing group of newly reported HIV/AIDS cases is African-American women and young adults. This does not imply that we are more likely to get HIV/AIDS than other groups. HIV/AIDS research data available from the CDC is from public agencies and providers who generally provide services to uninsured populations. Nevertheless, we have to be proactive in securing our future. Many women are contracting the disease through heterosexual activities from our men.

"It is inexcusable that a preventable disease has taken over our mind, body, and soul, as well as our communities. Something as simple as protected sex can reduce the likelihood of HIV/AIDS. Like you, Kenya, women trust their mates so much or do not care about themselves. Alternatively, we are so desperate to please a man that we neglect ourselves in the process. The heck with these numbers that say the ratio is 1:16 men available for women. Who cares when your life is on the line?"

Ebony continues, "So, Kenya, it does not matter that he says that he will never do it again. The fact of the matter is, he exposed himself to a same-sex relationship and thereby exposed you to the possibility of HIV/AIDS." "Well, Ebony, you are right, and I did not know if I should believe him, because he tried to make me believe that those initials belonged to a woman." Ebony interjected and said, "Well, whether a homothug or gay person, they are all a 'she', so technically he did not lie when he said the initials belonged to a woman." Kenya said, "Ebony, please! Stop and listen."

"Seriously, Kenya, there are many ways a woman can be pleasing unto herself without being subject to HIV/AIDS and death. We must learn to live celibate lives and abstain from sexual relationships until married, and if we cannot wait, then we ought to engage in protected sex, and that includes oral sex, which most men and women think is different. The schools and churches give you one alternative or the other, however, life is not that simple and sex safe must be the message to implement with teaching abstinence. It is unfortunate that people produce movies and write books about one-night stands and ninety-day rules without educating people about safe sex. Especially, African

American women who represent a greater portion of the publicly reported HIV/AIDS data. Nevertheless, wives have to be proactive in protecting their bodies from this disease."

Kenya said, "Well, he told me that God had changed him and that he wanted to be changed and did not want a divorce. He said his sin is no different than seeking forgiveness for any other sin. He appeared baffled by the decision of the world to condemn homosexuality, but embrace predators and murderers. He could not understand how prisoners who have committed vile offenses receive a pat on the back and welcome back to God embraces from the church. Alternatively, homosexuality is the sin of all sin. He understood that the Bible says it is an abomination. However, he is baffled about why people are not forgiving when a man desires to change his ways. He said that the book of Ezekiel 18:21-24 says, in pertinent part, that 'if a wicked man turns away from all the sins he has committed and keeps all my [God] decrees and does what is just and right, he will surely live; he will not die. None of the offenses he has committed will be remembered against him. Because of the righteous things he has done, he will live.'" Ebony interjected, saying, "He has some nerve, he is gay, and now he wants to quote the Bible?" "Ebony, I said the same thing," replied Kenya.

"He said that so-called Christians operate in hate and division and use the scriptures for their own agenda. I told him once gay, always gay! He said that is not true. He said, 'Kenya, some men try different things. They explore everything from interracial dating to different sexual acts, to experiencing with men or more than one woman at a time. Some men watch women perform sexual acts, and some women watch their husbands or boyfriends perform acts with two women.' He asked, 'Is she gay?' I responded, 'Yes. Yes, she is gay or crazy!' I told him that he was making excuses." Kenya exclaims, "Then he had the audacity to say that homosexuality is not about sex for most men or lesbian women, it is a relationship between two people of the same sex, which is about companionship and love, and not just sex. So he says!"

Ebony interjected, "You let him confuse you with that mess." Kenya said, "If that is confusing, check this out, he said that homosexuals engage in sexual acts with each other for many reasons that include mental illness; a way of life if they are homeless or on drugs; for sexual prowess; as a fad in order to try something new; and because they believe that they were born that way." Mahogany said, "What was your response to his comments, Kenya?"

I responded and said if it is an illness, then they can seek help, see a medical doctor, psychiatrist, or psychologist. If they are homeless or are on drugs, help is available because there are shelters, family, friends, and/or low-paying jobs that can keep them off the street. There are drug treatment programs for those who choose to change, and I know that they are not available everywhere, but they do exist. It is inexcusable to be so-called gay for sexual prowess, that is, to engage in the rape of another man during incarceration or purposefully and intentionally try to turn someone out. This occurs from the dudes that rape in prison to take someone's manhood in order to satisfy their own needs. I went on to say if it is due to a so-called fad, then the fad can be changed. Fads are temptation, and such urges are subject to prayer and deliverance for the disciplined person, or they can seek spiritual or medical help. Last, if it is a lifestyle for someone who believes that they were born that way, God does not make any mistakes. Unlike the white and Asian community, some African American and Latinos deal with homosexuality from a different premise. It appears that whites and Asians promote political, social and economic agendas like marriage, civil unions, adoptions, equal rights and awareness. Unfortunately, for some African Americans and Latinos, we see more flamers, fashion trend setter and issues between heterosexual women and gay men. Within the community the focus seems more on sexual prowess and less on social, political and economic reform.

"I continued telling him what I thought about his behavior and his sexual orientation. I asked, 'Is it the desire to be with someone of the same-sex for sexual pleasure; is it having mannerisms of the opposite sex? What is 'that way', because God created us in His image, and He is not homosexual? Considering every reason that He has described, there are no excuses for this type of behavior,' I replied. "Therefore, if you feel you have an abnormality, help is available if you choose to use it. I continued our dialogue and said, 'The problem is, most people do not want help,' and I told him that included him. It is easier to say God made a mistake in His creation or that they were born that way, rather than recognize that they were born male and that their sexual desires toward other men are just that, desires! I told him, 'Once gay, always gay, it is a lifestyle of choice,' I replied. He disagreed but could not really explain himself other than to seek forgiveness and say that he is a changed man and did not want a divorce.

"He began yelling and exclaiming, 'If you never learned this about me, I would be the same man today that I was when we dated and first married.' 'Yes, you are correct, a lying, gay man operating on the D.L.!' I replied. Girl, I started yelling scriptures from the Bible." Mahogany interjects, "I was waiting to hear how you were going to deal with that demon spirit." "Well, I quoted from the Book of Romans, 1:24 -32, the part that says, 'men committed indecent acts with other men, and received in themselves the due penalty for their perversion.' I also quoted from First Corinthians 5:9–13 and Chapter 6: 9–10, which says homosexual offenders will not inherit the Kingdom of God. I got loud, and he got louder. He cried and asked me the meaning of the book of Ezekiel 18: 21-24.

40

"He asked me if I believed that God delivered him from homosexuality. On the other hand, that God did not deliver him from sin. He said, 'Kenya, Romans 10:9 says that if I confess with my mouth, Jesus is Lord and believe in my heart that God raised him from the dead, I will be saved.' Furthermore, he said that he would enter heaven before the so-called Christians who bust down the church doors and fast every day, but have hate in their heart and are self-righteous. 'Kenya,' he demanded, 'God is a just God. He has mercy and compassion on whomever believes and has faith in Him. He has mercy and compassion,' quoting Romans 9:14-21. 'Why bother living for God if He will judge us for our past deeds and will not forgive us?' He continued making his case and said, 'Kenya, are you saying that God can raise Jesus from the dead, but cannot deliver me from homosexuality? God forgave me, and you will not. Kenya, you need to read Psalms 103:3 and Ephesians 4:32.' He continued with his plea, saying that he has been faithful to me and that this incident was from his past. 'So you say,' I replied. I walked away and slept in my daughter's room.

"The next morning, my mother called me into her room and said she could not help but hear my conversation with my husband. She vowed never to interfere with my marriage or relationships, she believes that matters of the heart should be resolved between the parties and that family, friends and outsiders should mind their own business unless violence, drugs and abuse is in the relationship. However, she said that I needed to pray about the questions he posed. She said, 'What would happen to all the men who prayerfully desired deliverance from homosexuality, but cannot find refuge with a woman? God is and continues to be a forgiving God,' she said, 'what about you? Do you believe that God can raise Jesus from the dead but cannot deliver a homosexual from bondage? God can do all things, he formed us in His image, and He formed the heavens and the earth. If your husband said that he is delivered from homosexuality and you have no proof stating otherwise, then trust and believe in God that he is telling you the truth.' I responded to my mother by saying, 'Mommy, pastors teach us that homosexuality is a very strong demon spirit and that women should not continue in relationships with men known to us to be gay.' 'I agree, but your husband is saying that he has received deliverance from this bondage and has not been in a homosexual relationship since his college days.

'A homosexual spirit may be too much for a pastor, but nothing is too hard for God.' She told me to read Luke 9:1 and 10:17. My mother asked me whether my thoughts about homosexuality would be different if he were subject to sexual abuse by another man during his childhood and adolescent years. In addition, whether I would consider him gay for having a sexual relationship if it were not consensual; she asked whether my thoughts would be different if he were released from prison and shared a prison rape story or conveyed that he engaged in prison sex, so-called survival sex. She wanted to know whether I was concerned about his same-sex experience or his same-sex relationship. I did not know how to answer her, because I believe any form of same-sex relationship is gay in form, and it does not matter whether it is sexual, emotional, and/or physical. The thought of my husband being in the arms of another man is too much for me to handle.

"She left me with this thought, why do people use the Bible to justify homosexuality as a sin, but refuse to recite the Bible to live in love, peace and harmony? The same Bible that teaches about homosexuality and sin also teaches about repentance, love, mercy, grace, understanding, and forgiveness."

Seven

THE POWER OF PRAYER

Ebony asked what happened next. "Unbelievably, Ebony, when I called you, I wanted all of us to conference on the phone and pray. Now, we are here in Atlanta. Well, let us pray, but first let us pray for Sahara," Mahogany led the prayer.

"Father God, in the name of Jesus, according to Your purpose, plan, and will, according to Your Word in Matthew 14:14, Isaiah 54:17, Jeremiah 33:6, 3 John: 21 and Mark 1:4, heal Sahara. God, You know her infirmities, touch her now, in Jesus' name. We bind up sickness, disease, and death. We stand on Your Word. Amen.

"Now, Father, You can do all things, You are the same God today as yesterday and forever. We lift up Kenya and her husband, we believe that when a man and a woman come together, let no man put asunder. We know their thoughts are not Your thoughts and their ways are not Your ways, as proclaimed in Isaiah 55:6–11, we know that Your Word will not return void, but will accomplish what You set out for it to do. God, let her not be put to shame, disgrace, and humiliation, as proclaimed in Isaiah 54:4 and Psalm 25:2. We know You will keep her in perfect peace because her mind is steadfast and she trusts in You, according to Isaiah 26:3. God, keep her in Your secret place, according to Psalm 91. Lord, give her wisdom, according to Isaiah 48:17, Proverbs 14 and 31. We stand on Your Word – Amen."

After praying, Kenya exclaimed that she was relieved but still confused about her husband's behavior and his failure to share his homosexual experience. She wondered if his same sex relationship was the reason why he patiently waited for her until they were married; he did not push her into having premarital sex. Ebony said that should have been a sign. "I mean, it is fine for a man to respect your spirituality, but sometimes that may be a sign that something else is going on. I know we learn about fornication, but heck, if a man does not make a pass at you or try to kiss you, lick you or do something, then that may be a sign of something greater than patiently waiting for marriage. Heck, even a dog will lick your face. Maybe it indicates that he is getting sex from someone or somewhere else or that he is not into women. Alternatively, he is into men. Maybe it means that he respects you, your values and morals, and his walk with God. Kenya, do you remember when you were in school and I asked you whether you spent time with his friends?" "Yes, I remember."

Ebony asked, "Do you also remember when Mahogany suggested that you attend one of their fishing or hunting trips and you said that he told you that those trips were for the 'boys' only? Well, it is strange that a man, whether husband or boyfriend, would preclude or prevent his wife or girlfriend from interacting with his friends or having them to the home for dinner or something. At some point in time, a woman should stop and question why the men in her husband or boyfriend's life are a secret. What is he really hiding? Too often, women look for the other woman in his life, but we should be as focused on the men in his life. If we really look, we will see the signs. If not, every girl should have a gay male friend who with two snaps can spot a gay dude and call him out." "You are right, Ebony. I just do not know what to do now." "Well, Kenya, keep the matter in prayer, and do not lean on anyone's understanding, let God be your guide." "You are right, Mahogany."

"Proverbs 13:7 says one man pretends to be rich, yet has nothing; another pretends to be poor, yet has great wealth. You know, there is nothing worse than pretending around friends. There should never be a moment when friends, true friends, have to maintain an image." Kenya said, "This was truly a SHE (Sharing Her Experience) moment for me! Now, all of this talking and crying has made sista girl hungry!" "Oh, I have to call Ms. Hopkins for Diamond, we have to bring her to the cafeteria," said Mahogany. "Okay," replied Kenya and Ebony. Diamond arrived at the hospital, and the women took her to the gift shop. Thereafter, they ate and laughed together in the cafeteria. Diamond asked Mahogany, "Auntie, when is Mommy coming home? I miss her." Mahogany replied, "Soon, very soon. You know what, Diamond? If you pray to God, He will hear your prayer." Diamond wanted to know what she should say to God. Ebony showed Diamond how to pray. She threw her little hands into the air to pray. Ebony suggested, "Tell God how much you miss your Mommy and how much you want her home. Tell Him you believe that He can heal her and make her better." Diamond repeated the prayer and said, "Now I know that God is going to bring my mommy home." Then, Ms. Hopkins asked if they spoke with the doctor. Kenya replied, "You know, that is odd, because all of the time that we spent in the room, we did not see the doctor after our initial visit. The nurse came by the room, but not the doctor."

Ebony, remembering her conversation with the hospital representative, said, "After we eat, each of us should call the doctor and individually go to the nurses' station and inquire about his visitation and her condition. Kenya, since you are in the profession, go to the chief of staff and tell them we have been here all morning and afternoon, and no attending physician has visited with Sahara, and she is in ICU." They did exactly what Ebony recommended. Shortly thereafter, the doctor made his rounds. Ironic, Ms. Hopkins was visiting with Sahara when he arrived. Ebony and Kenya were finishing their conversation at the nurses' station, and they had already called the chief of staff. Mahogany was with Diamond, taking a walk. They concluded visitation and went back to the hotel. The next morning, they headed out to the hospital. Mahogany's cell phone rang. She missed the call, and the caller left no message for her. Nervous, she called the hospital to inquire about Sahara, but the nurse said that she could not give out any information over the phone and instructed her to come to the hospital immediately. Upon arrival, they learned that Sahara was conscious and breathing on her own. They asked if she could speak, and the nurse said yes but warned them that she was unconscious for several days. The nurse continued saying that although her vital signs were normal, her doctor wanted to keep her in ICU to monitor her. "Please do not overwhelm her. You may go in one at a time, so she will not react. As a cautionary note, patients can be frightened and think the worse when they see so many family members and friends upon regaining consciousness." They thanked the nurse for her input.

They obliged and visited one-by-one, Kenya first, then Mahogany and then Ebony. When they thought that everything was okay, they all entered the room together and sat around. Sahara asked about Diamond. She said that she had a vision of Diamond praying with three angels. They all smiled. Sahara asked when did they arrive, and Kenya said a few days ago. She said, "Wow, y'all came down here for me. What did y'all do, just watch me? I bet I look a mess." Ebony said, "I bet you did, but we bathed you and did your hair." "Here, look in the mirror," said Kenya. "You look great, considering." "Do not lie to her," Ebony said, "you look like you have been in a deep sleep." "Well, what did the doctor say about me?" asked Sahara. "Nothing, and we did not ask," replied Kenya. "Ebony, you did not ask?" "No, Sahara, this trip has taught me a lot, and how you got here is not important. I am more concerned with how you leave." "What! Well, that is a good look, and thank you," Sahara replied, smiling.

Seeing the nurse at the door, Sahara said, "Well, here is the nurse." She asked the nurse, "Do I have to take it via needle?" "Yes, the doctor will continue your insulin via needle until your blood sugar is okay." The nurse told Sahara that she is very lucky because she could have gone into a diabetic coma. Mahogany replied, "Well, we do not believe in luck, we believe in blessings." "So do I, but I cannot share my beliefs on the job," replied the nurse. Lyrically, Ebony said, "By your works, you can." The nurse said, "So I guess I can tell you that God had an angel watching over this woman all of the time. I was passing through the ER when I saw her little daughter crying. I asked her what was wrong, and she said that her mommy was sick and that she called 911 to get her help. Finger pointing, the little girl said that she heard the woman over there say that her mommy did not have insurance. 'What does that mean?' she asked me. I told her not to worry about that, because her mommy was safe.

"I asked if she had someone here, and she said she has her Auntie Mahogany's number and she gave it to me, and that was how I called. She told me where she went to school, and I called a friend who is a teacher in the area to see if she knew of a teacher at that school. She said she knew Ms. Hopkins. She called her for me, and she offered to come over to the hospital to get Diamond. Diamond is her student, and she is very familiar with her mother. Since there was no family, I thought that was better than calling Social Services and placing her in their care for the night. I knew that she was going to be okay, my husband is an E.R. physician, and he was her attending doctor." She concluded by saying, "You have done a wonderful job raising Diamond. I hear that you are also in school." "Yes, I am in my last semester of undergraduate studies," replied Sahara.

Eight

THE HEALING STARTS NOW

Sahara said, "I am so grateful that you did not call Social Services; they are the reason why I was stressing and not eating. They claimed their psychologist, which by the way they forced me to take her to, said my daughter suffered from Hyperactive and Attention Deficiency Disorder and needed to be medicated. Her former school social worker said the same. I refuted their accusations about her needing medicine, because Diamond is in a new school now and she is performing well, and I will not give her any medicine. They have been pursuing this medication issue for months. The psychologist prescribed her medicine for her disorder, and for depression. I thought it was unethical for him to prescribe this for a child of her age. I requested research on these drugs and the other drugs that doctors prescribe in high numbers to our children, but he did not have any. I wanted to read what the long-term effects were, especially for girls. He did not have any research and said to his knowledge no research existed. I know many children, especially in the African-American community, who are on these types of drugs. This is especially true of our boys. I told him that I knew of several boys on anti-psychotic medication for the treatment of bi-polar disorder and conduct disorders. The children are worse now than before they were medicated."

Ebony said, "Unfortunately, the mothers do not ask questions, or they simply do not know what to ask.

Moreover, many of them get Social Services checks or disability checks for their children, and some prefer the check to assuring the best for their children. The children begin to believe that they are disabled and do not perform academically, and they give up socially. Part of the school-to-prison pipeline starts with special needs children and placement in special education classes. As soon as these children misbehave, the school suspends them. Then, the children go from the schoolhouse, to the courthouse, and to the jailhouse to be in a warehouse. No treatment or rehabilitation is available, and mental health services aren't available. Some of the children experience sexual abuse by the staff and other inmates. Imagine removing a child from their home, school and community for months because of talking back to a teacher, talking in class (also called disrupting the school), or having a cat fight at school. When we were growing up, we acted the same way, but no one medicated us or incarcerated us."

Ebony continued and said, "In fact, they said I had behavioral and mental problems, but I was never medicated, and I turned out great. Medicating children is a new drug trade, only now the children are so young, and when they get older, they will be addicted to controlled substance drugs. Furthermore, we do not know if they will get older; by the time Diamond reaches 18, she could have problems with her brain, lungs, or kidneys, etc. Furthermore, suicide among our children has drastically increased, and I wonder if there is a connection between these medicines and suicide. Clinical social workers and psychologists should not be able to prescribe drugs; these people are experimenting with our children and using them as lab rats. In fact, other children suffer as well as African-American children."

Mahogany asked, "Sahara, what is the Department of Family and Children Services trying to do?" Sahara replied, "DFACS is forcing me to medicate her. They are saying if I do not give her the medication that the doctor prescribed that they can file a petition of neglect against me and place her in foster care." Crying, Sahara says, "I do not want her in foster care, but she does not need the medicine. There is nothing wrong with my baby. She was hyperactive for a while, but over the last year, since we moved into the house, she has stability and is doing extremely well in school. I have changed her diet, eating habits and sleep." Ebony said, "But she is only five?" The nurse asked, "Do you have a lawyer?" Sahara said no. "They said that the judge would appoint me a lawyer upon filing the petition. Money is tight for me right now, and I am really trying to do right by Diamond." Ebony said, "You need your own lawyer, and I will pay for it. Bunk a court appointed attorney; you will be lucky if you see them before your scheduled hearing."

"Okay, Sahara, you are going to be fine," the nurse said, "and I wish I had good friends like you. Well, the doctor wants to observe you for 24-48 hours, and thanks to your friends, he is not taking any chances." Sahara wanted to know if they were staying at her place. "No. We are at a hotel," replied Ebony. "Are you all too good to stay at my place?" "No, it is not that." "So what is going on?" "Okay, tonight we will stay at your place. That will mean a lot to Diamond and I. Now, let me call Diamond."

Nine

PAST, PRESENT AND FUTURE

Sahara really wanted Ebony to stay at her home. She knew what Ebony thought about her. Therefore, she wanted her to see that she was doing well for herself and Diamond. She was anxious to tell Ebony that she lived in the Cascade area of Southeast Atlanta. It is a beautiful, affluent community by any standards and is a haven for many successful African-Americans. Sahara said, "You know, contrary to what many people think about strippers, we do not always waste our money. Some of us are aware that we have a chance to meet and interact with wealthy men who desire women like us. Ebony, I learned a lot from you about money and investments. You are a drill sergeant. I saved for a down payment to buy the house and to give Diamond a safe community with great schools. My credit is very good, and I started a college fund for Diamond."

Ebony said, "Well, since you are up to talking, please tell me why you are still stripping." "Girl, I stopped stripping two years ago. I collapsed one night, and that is how I found out that I was diabetic. I do not drink or do drugs anymore. The medication and drinking can kill me." Laughing, Sahara said, "Honestly, I cannot strip while I am sober. Anyway, it has been a long road. I had a lot of money saved up for the house but was living with somebody who was keeping Diamond and I; you know what I am saying? Therefore, she was not doing well in school, and we were having problems.

I decided to get right with God and take a step of faith. I moved out, bought the house and we are okay. She is doing great in school, and that matters a lot to me. I was in that life for a long time, and other than diabetes, I do not have any other diseases or anything, you know. I have received many blessings. Let no one fool you, you cannot make money just stripping. You might have to turn tricks. Some of us have addictions to drugs or alcohol. Therefore, you will do whatever you need to in order to support the habit. You either turn tricks or are tricked! Trick, Whore, Treat! We trick to get treats. However, I know many sisters and brothers who got caught out there big time with STDs, AIDS, and drugs. People's homes are destroyed or will be destroyed when their wives find out what their husbands have done. They think that we are stupid, but we keep pictures with our cell phones, and we record their activities. We have video footage of them at hotels, as well as other places. From pastors to entertainers, to everyday survivors, a lot of them have caught the 'package'.

"I know a girl that lives here in Atlanta. We call her a homegirl. A baller saved her, but she got AIDS. He is so stupid, because he does not know about her ordeal. He never asked her to get a test. Wait, check this out, she is bi-sexual, and her companion is a stripper who runs around with married men and women. The baller is married and lives out of state, she says that he refuses to use a condom with her. He is into everything! They think they got game, but they play themselves every day! The girls want to be a homegirl to this or that person. You cannot tell the dudes anything, they know it all, or they believe that it will not happen to them.

"What in the world do you think will happen to you if you are cutting with a stripper? We tell all of them the same thing, that they are the only one. When they leave town, the next plane lands and we got out our hands! We work the out-of-towners and the locals. They refuse to use condoms, but I told them, you had better use condomsense!" Laughing aloud, Sahara says, "They do not think about their wives or significant others. They make babies, and some of them do not tell their wives or girlfriends about it because their agents make monthly payments. There are some who threaten us to have abortions with all of sorts of stuff. The number of abortions is crazy high." Ebony interjects, "Not to mention that since 1973, African Americans aborted millions of African American children at a rate of almost 1,452 per day."

Sahara continued, saying, "The men are wealthy, so most of us are scared. Some of them refuse to do right at all, and women are running them down for child support. So much goes on in that life. We will not even talk about the down-low and homo-thugs. They come to the club so we can hook them up with men (laughing). Sista girl, please, you will be surprised as to the number of pastors and ministers, and ballers and entertainers who are on the D.L., and it is sad. Nevertheless, we just want them to pay us for our services. We are not social workers, so we do not say anything. They are just ATM machines that we use to get money.

"I am not glorifying my past lifestyle. Deuteronomy 11:26 and chapter twenty-eight say choose this day life or death, blessings or curses. I thought that I chose blessings because it was monetary gain, but I did not have peace and joy. Many nights, I did not know if I would have a roof over my head or whether they would kick me out or ask me to do something that I did not feel comfortable doing. Moreover, if I turn a trick and got killed or gang raped, who would take care of my daughter?

On the other hand, whether I would overdose and die in the street like a dog because someone would be too scared to report it, or whether I would suffer from a disease. My greatest fear was whether someone would hurt my daughter. I only found peace and joy when I allowed God to enter my life; He was there waiting for me to say yes! I have a problem with ministries that talk about prosperity, because many people equate prosperity to blessings. Blessings and prosperity to me is that I do not lack, God meets all of my needs. There are things that I want and desire, but I do not need them. I do not have what others may have, but I am blessed! Now that I am out of that life, I know it was nothing but the grace of God that truly saved me. No man 'saved' me. God is my savior. I received counseling to address my childhood abuse. Now, I am okay. In fact, I think that I am doing great."

"Well, Sahara, you need health insurance." "I know, Ebony." "I am going to get you and Diamond coverage." "Really! Ebony. Thank you!" "The billing department told me that there are several major insurance companies down here that offer coverage at reasonable rates for you and Diamond. In fact, one of them is the same company that I use for the business, so I will inquire of them first. With diabetes, you need needles, insulin, and have to attend regular doctor appointments, etc. The nurse said that you need testing equipment. I will commit to get it for you, at least a two-year supply. I am so proud of you for being in school and getting a house, I really am. Nevertheless, I am concerned about what would happen to Diamond if Ms. Hopkins did not get her. Who is down here to help you?" Sahara started crying. Kenya said, "Ebony, we are not here to get her worked up." "Well, I just want her to know that she does not need to pretend with us, she does not have to maintain an image, because we are her family. Just keep it real!" Ebony replied.

Ebony continued questioning Sahara, asking, "Are you current with your mortgage? You said that money was tight." "No," replied Sahara. "I have stock options, and I will help you with your mortgage for twelve months to give you a chance to get work after graduation. You have always been smart, so you will be teaching in no time." "It's $1480.00 per month, and I owe two months. It would help Diamond and I a lot if you could make that commitment," said Sahara. "Is the information in your home?" "Yes, Ebony, it is in the top drawer of the nightstand in my bedroom. I guess that is how I got sick, I am going through so much." Crying, Sahara said, "I am really trying!"

Mahogany told Sahara, "The devil is mad at you because you stopped stripping and are living for God. That is why he is trying to afflict your body in order to force you into debt. He wants you to return to your old lifestyle for monetary support. Nevertheless, the devil is a liar. God allowed you to collapse so that He could pull you out of that life, so that you would stop stripping, drinking and doing drugs. God will provide all of your needs, and even though you did not have health insurance, he still covered you and gave you everything that you needed. He will continue to give you everything according to His purpose, plan, and will. We know that we are in a recession, and when it hits your front door, it is a depression. Nevertheless, it is important for people to remain focused and remember from whence their help comes. Oftentimes, financial crisis makes people stronger, builds character and most importantly bonds family and friendships.

"We need to remember MVR, our morals, values and respect. This is the driving force that should direct our path and control our destiny. Too often, we lose ourselves in trying times and fall. This is the time when loved ones should be helping each other and family and friends should move in with each other and do what we did in the old days when first, second and third generations lived together. Back then, families helped each other and stayed with each other through thick and thin. Now marriages are falling apart, and at the first glance of trouble, people are divorcing, friendships are dissolving and people are crumbling. God uses these trying times to rebuild family, friends, and finances through faith."

Ten

THE GIFT OF REAL FRIENDS

They left the hospital for Sahara's house and picked up Diamond along the way. Upon arrival, the women were all astonished to see that Sahara did not have any furniture, her bed was on the floor with no frame or box spring, but her closet was full of clothing. Diamond's bed had a mattress, box spring and a frame. Kenya started crying and said, "At least she has a place of her own to call home, and she is trying to get her life in order and attend school." Kenya decided that she would purchase Diamond and Sahara a bedroom suit as a housewarming present, by charging it to her account and paying it off when she returned home. However, she wanted to get permission from her husband first. She called her husband to see if it was okay, because he does not like debt and the card is for emergencies only. He agreed, and he offered in the alternative to send her money via wire. However, she said she would not know the cost until she went to the store, and the use of the card for that limited purpose would be ideal. He told her to pay it off from their savings account when she returned home.

Ebony interjected and said, "Kenya, he believes in cash only transactions because you cannot trace what he does, if he is at a hotel or not, or if he purchases items for someone else, etc. So be mindful of his cash-only approach to saving and using money." Kenya said she never thought about it that way, but she would give it thought. In the meantime, Ebony searched the nightstand drawer and came across dozens of past due utility bills. Mahogany agreed to pay for those bills. She arranged to go to the post office before closing to get money orders and mail the payments. Kenya asked that they make a mental note to tell Sahara to ask for budget billing, payment plans so that she could be current with her payments and know what to expect every month. Ebony suggested that they make a mental note to tell Sahara to disconnect either the cell phone or the home phone until her income improved. Ebony placed a call to the mortgage company to request their city and state code to send the money by wire. The account information was on the coupons, and information about ACH/Debit from the checking account was on the letter from the mortgage company advising of foreclosure. She decided to immediately bring the account current and then await Sahara's release to arrange for the checking account debit plan. With that done, Ebony agreed to surprise Sahara with furniture for the house.

Ebony said, "Girlfriend has struggled most of her life, and purchasing furniture is a great idea. However, we should not purchase items too fancy, just to meet her needs." She said, "Let Diamond pick out her own princess-styled bedroom suit. Let us see if we can get these items delivered before she comes home." Kenya agreed and said, "We need to wait for Mahogany to come back with the car." Upon Mahogany's return, they all headed to the furniture store. Diamond was so excited that she found herself a beautiful princess bedroom suit. Kenya found a canopy mahogany rice poster bed, with dresser, mirror, and nightstand. Ebony found the leather sectional that will be perfect for the great room, and Mahogany picked out two pairs of breakfast bar chairs and a dinette set. The store agreed to deliver the following day. They each agreed to pay for their own gifts.

Later that evening, Kenya overheard Ebony on the telephone with her business associate, discussing her health.

Kenya asked Ebony about her health, and Ebony assured her that she was fine. She told Ebony she overheard her discussing liquidating some of her assets and paying off secured debts. However, Ebony brushed off the conversation as nothing more than a mere business decision, nothing more.

Eleven

WHAT EVERY LITTLE GIRL SHOULD HAVE

Diamond was so excited about her new furniture purchase that she could not sleep. She stayed awake all night, trying to help her aunties clean. She told her Auntie Mahogany about the 24-hour grocery store for food. Realizing that no one ate, Mahogany agreed to go grocery shopping, and she wanted to locate a place to eat. Ebony agreed the Camp Creek area had many nice places to eat that were conveniently located close to the house for a quick meal. The following day, Ebony remained at the house to await the delivery of the furniture. Diamond begged to stay home, but she received instructions to go to school and be surprised when she came home. The company delivered the furniture as scheduled. The girls wanted to know what to do with the other items, and Ebony requested that they place them in the third bedroom. Further, she asked Kenya if she minded picking up new bed linens and comforters. Kenya agreed but said she was exhausted. Kenya laughed about sleeping on the floor and said she did not have a good night's sleep.

After lunchtime, they returned to the hospital and saw that Sahara was not in her room and that a nursing assistant was changing the bedding. Kenya spoke to her and said the patient in this room had died. Hysterical, Kenya ran down the hall to make contact with Mahogany. She told Mahogany that Sahara had died, exclaiming, "She is dead! She is dead! Why did God do that?" Numb and in disbelief, Mahogany said God does not make mistakes. She said that Sahara was at peace, the peace that she yearned for so much in this lifetime. Proverbs 14:30 says, "A heart at peace gives life to the body." She lived to enjoy that peace, saying that some people never receive it in their lifetime. "Furthermore, we were here with her and Diamond, and she knows that Diamond will be all right. By the way, did you find a will when you all were going through her belongings yesterday? Sahara does not have a family, and she did not want Diamond in foster care." Kenya was too distraught to answer Mahogany.

Kenya fell to her knees, screaming and crying in the hallway. Although Mahogany felt heartache, she also felt a sense of peace. Ebony and Mahogany wanted to know whether Sahara had a will with a guardianship provision that disclosed who has guardianship over Diamond. Ebony said, "Too often, single mothers do not think about guardianships. They do not consider what will happen to their children when they die. The fact of the matter is that their children are in court battles between the maternal and paternal sides of the family." Again, Ebony asked, "Do you know if she has a will with a guardianship provision so we can take care of Diamond?" However, Kenya was not trying to hear anything at that point, because she was in disbelief. Mahogany told Kenya, "I have a peace that passes all understanding." Kenya reached out and placed her hand over Mahogany's mouth and said, "Not now, not now, please be quiet." Mahogany said, "Listen to me. I feel a peace that passes all understanding, and we are going to pray about this together, get up right now." "Mahogany, I know you have strong faith, but sometimes you have to know when to turn it down and be silent." "Kenya, God intended for faith to be experienced. I said I have a peace that passes all understanding." "Okay! Mahogany! Okay!"

Kenya stood up, and Mahogany began to cry out to the Lord, declaring that she needed Him to speak concerning her peace. "Surely, Lord, I do not understand this type of peace upon the death of a friend, I do not understand this feeling, it's not closure for me, please minister to me, Lord." While they were praying, the same nurse who had attended to Sahara and saw her upon admission approached them, smiling. Kenya asked her why was she smiling. The nurse recognized that Kenya and Mahogany were crying and asked what was wrong. They responded that the CNA said that Sahara died. The nurse said, "No, no, no, that is incorrect." "What!" Kenya wanted to know if Sahara had died and came back to life. "No! I just took her downstairs. She is waiting for you all to pick her up at the front entrance," the nurse replied. "I went with the orderly and took her downstairs so that I could converse with her on her way out. No one died here," the nurse exclaimed. "The CNA was merely asked to prepare the room for another patient, that is customary practice. You know that, Kenya, you are a nurse." "The CNA said that the patient died." "Well, I am so sorry that you had this horrible experience."

Mahogany said, "Lord, thank you for an answered prayer." Kenya said, "That was the peace that you had, Mahogany. You knew that she was not dead, that was why you said you did not have closure, right?" Mahogany responded, "I knew something was different, and God tested us." Kenya demanded an explanation. "You know, you wanted to believe that God raised Sahara from the dead, but you still doubt that He can deliver your husband from homosexuality?" "My faith was also tested, Kenya. It is easy as an evangelist to give advice to others. However, today I had to trust God for myself. The nurse said that no one died here, but someone did." Kenya asked, "Who, Mahogany?" "We did. We died here this week. A part of all of us died here. Our image of life is shattered, but not broken. Although the cares of this life matter, the love of God does not fade, and it does not shatter."

Twelve

BREAKTHROUGH

Kenya and Mahogany rushed down the stairs to get Sahara. They hugged and kissed her and were tired from crying earlier. Sahara said, "Are y'all okay?" They both responded that they were great! They elected not to share the incident with Sahara immediately. When they reached home, the beautiful furnishings in her home took Sahara by surprise. She was so excited. Ms. Hopkins dropped Diamond off after school, and Ebony cooked. They all gathered and counted their blessings! Ebony had developed a nagging cough that seemingly got worse during her stay in Atlanta. Kenya asked her if she was okay, and she replied that she was fine. Ms. Hopkins prepared to leave to go home, and they all thanked her for her generosity. Before leaving, Diamond gave her a gift and a card. Sahara whispered to Ebony, "That was your fault." Ebony smiled and said, "No, it was yours. Your daughter asked me if she could pick something out for her teacher who helped her and her mommy. I saw that beautiful picture and thought that she would like it, but your daughter saw it first. Like you, she, too, has expensive taste." Both of them laughed.

Days later, Sahara's health was returning, so she returned to school. She also hired an attorney and a private psychiatrist for Diamond's case against DFACS/CPS. In addition, she was current with her mortgage and other expenses. Therefore, Kenya, Ebony, and Mahogany decided to leave. Ebony left Sahara an envelope, and it contained enough cash to hold her over for a while. Each of them continued to stay in touch with the other. About three months later, Kenya was concerned that no one had heard from Ebony. She called Sahara and Mahogany and learned that they had not spoken with Ebony during the last few days. Sahara said she presumed that Ebony was at a conference or on business travel. They called her cell, office, and home numbers. They realized that no one had any other forms of contact for her, no information on her mother's address or telephone number, or a friend in Texas. Kenya called directory assistance to search for a listing for Ebony's mother. There was no listing. She called directory assistance to get the main number for Ebony's business. When she called and spoke with the receptionist, the receptionist informed her that Ebony had passed away a week earlier. Kenya tried to be strong, because she thought that this could be a false alarm. Hoping that the woman would respond in the negative, she asked the receptionist for any information about the family or funeral. Instead, the woman told her where they funeralized Ebony. Astonished, Kenya began screaming and crying aloud.

Kenya called her husband while her mother comforted her. Mahogany called the receptionist and demanded a telephone number for the nearest family member or the funeral home. The receptionist gave Mahogany a number to the funeral home only. Mahogany called the funeral home, and the director asked about her relationship with Ebony. She responded that they were like sisters. He told her that he funeralized Ebony last week. To his knowledge, Ebony died after suffering from an illness. He referred Mahogany to Ebony's business associate. Mahogany requested to get information about Ebony's mother. The director said to his knowledge, Ebony did not have any family, and she did not have a mother. Mahogany immediately called Ebony's business associate.

Pearl told Mahogany that Ebony died from lupus or sarcoidosis, an illness that affects the immune system. She noted that this illness is prevalent amongst African-Americans and women, both young and old, and that some men have the disease. She said it is not HIV/AIDS and people cannot get it through sexual contact. To her knowledge, Ebony developed pneumonia while on a trip to Atlanta. She refused to get her nagging cough checked out by a doctor when she returned. Mahogany said, "Why did you not call us? I know that you had our information." "No, I swear I did not. I knew that she had close friends in different states, but I did not know your last names or addresses. I searched all over for her telephone book but never found it. She had a safe, but I did not have the access number." Mahogany asked, "Did you have her cell phone?" "I looked for it with hopes of finding numbers that she called." Pearl said, "We tried calling everyone else that we thought that she knew." "What about her mother and siblings, did you call them?" "Ebony did not have a mother or siblings. I have known her for at least 8 years since graduate school, and since we went into business. I know that she looked for them but never found them. She came to Texas in search of her family."

Pearl said, "I even asked a very close male acquaintance of hers if he knew how I could make contact with you all, and he said no. He said he heard of you all but did not have names and addresses. We looked for letters and anything that could have helped us." Mahogany said, "Well, obviously you did not look hard enough. If you looked at her email addresses and her telephone bill, you would have found us." "Mahogany, we did not have her password to get into her emails. We did not try to locate a phone bill; maybe if we did, we could have found your numbers," Pearl replied. "However, her friend, he said she did not have any family. I am so sorry, but we had no way of contacting any of you. Each of you are welcome to come by here to get a key to her home. I know how much she spoke of you, but I just did not have any last names or method of reaching you all. I am so very sorry!

"She had a wonderful funeral, and so many children came to show their respects. She was such a giving person. Just let me know when you all will come; in fact, I will put it on the company account if travel expenses are a problem. Alternatively, you can stay at her place, and you may be able to get into the safe." By now, both Kenya and Mahogany wanted Pearl to explain whether she had something in the safe. Pearl said, "No, and Ebony is very business oriented, so I assume that she will have a will." "What difference does that make now? You already buried her, Pearl?" "It was just a suggestion."

The news of Ebony's death stunned Mahogany, Kenya, and Sahara. They could not believe that their beloved friend was gone and they did not get to say goodbye. Eager to get to Texas, they flew out immediately. They stayed at Ebony's house. It was too late to go to the cemetery, so they went to sleep. Sahara had a dream; she saw Ebony at a safe in a room located in the basement. She saw Ebony open the safe and saw the numbers that she touched to open the safe. She immediately awoke everyone and said, "I just saw Ebony." Kenya and Mahogany were trying to figure out if there was some misunderstanding again concerning the death of a friend, so Kenya said, "What do you mean?" "I saw her in a dream." "What was she doing?" asked Mahogany. "She was opening a safe." "Are you serious?" exclaimed Mahogany. "Yes, why are you so anxious?"

Mahogany said, "Your dream is ironic, because Pearl, the business associate, said that there was a safe, but she did not have the number to get into it and they feared damaging the safe to get access to it." Kenya asked where she saw it. "I saw it in a room located in the basement." "There is no basement in this house," said Mahogany. "I know what I saw," replied Sahara. "What were the numbers? Maybe that will help," said Kenya. "I saw a combination of numbers and letters." Mahogany said, "Write them down here." Sahara wrote the information down on the paper. Kenya said, "Those numbers and letters look familiar, but I cannot place it." Sahara began to play with the letters and numbers and said, "Yes, it is us." "What do you mean?" "It is the first letters of our names," replied Sahara. "The numbers represent the date of each birthday. Remember she used to say that she was the only one with double digits in her birthday? Oh my God, now where is the basement?" Mahogany said. "Maybe God was showing you that it is downstairs, but not a basement. We are all upstairs, so maybe you saw a downstairs room with a closet." "Okay, Mahogany, maybe you are right. Let us go."

They went downstairs and realized that off the kitchen there was a beautifully decorated room with a closet. "Wow! This is beautiful," Sahara said. Kenya said lavender was her mother's favorite color. "She did this room in hopes of having a place for her mother." Kenya began crying. "Why didn't she tell us the truth? Why didn't she tell us that she never found her mother and siblings? Why didn't she tell us that she was sick? I asked her in Atlanta, and she said that she was fine." "I do not know, Kenya. Ebony was so proud. She held on to the only dignity that she had, she never escaped that night in New York when they took her from her mother and siblings." Then suddenly Mahogany said, "Quiet, stop, do you hear a noise?" "Yes, but where is it coming from?" replied Kenya. Sahara said, "I do not like the country and being out here alone. You need protection living out here." Mahogany said, "No weapon formed against us shall prosper, and God will keep us from evil." "Yeah, and a gun will keep away evil, too," Sahara replied. "Help her, Lord, because she does not understand what she is saying!" exclaimed Mahogany.

Mahogany said, "Shhhh! The noise is getting louder. Are you sure that Ebony is dead? Girl, I had my share of false alarms." Sahara said, "What are you saying?" "Long and short, the hospital told us that you died, and we lost it," replied Mahogany. Sahara asked, "When?" But Kenya did not want to focus on that issue, because she heard noises in the house. "Quiet!" The doorbell rung, and they all jumped, saying, "You get it!" "No, you get it." "Who knows that we are here?" asked Kenya. "Pearl may know. She left us the key, but no one told her when we were coming." "Let us go check," replied Mahogany. "It is an old woman at the door and a car waiting with the engine running. Open the door and see what she wants, Sahara." "No! People dress up, and when they get in, they rob you; it is a home invasion, no! You open it, Mahogany. What is in your spirit?" asked Sahara. "Jesus, Lord! Help them, God." Mahogany opened the door.

At the door, there stood an old African-American woman. Her hair was white, and she was wearing a dress coat with shoes. She had a floral arrangement in her hand. Floral arrangements were throughout the house. They recognized that the one in her hand resembled those around the house. They asked about her identity, and she told them that she was a member of the church that Ebony attended. Further, she worked for Ebony and lived there. She described the lavender bedroom and said that she was returning home after visiting with family in Kentucky. She said that she learned Ebony passed away and that Pearl, her business associate, had funeralized Ebony. She said she saw the light on and was scared to enter with her key because she did not know who was inside. Sahara asked her why she had a floral arrangement in her hand. She said because she makes them for Ebony every time she goes to visit with her family.

They asked her how she met Ebony. She said that many years ago, Ebony came to Texas looking for her mother and siblings. "I was working in janitorial services in the building that she bought to start her business. Ebony took ill one night, and I called for help. I stayed with her in the hospital and watched over her. I came by after work and checked on her every day. She got better and returned to work for her employer while she still managed her own business. She had some investment in her employer's company, and if I am correct, she made a lot of money with something called an IPO - Initial Public Offering, or something like that - and she became very wealthy. Some people buy a car, but that child retired me. I had been cleaning behind people for years, and I never had any children of my own. My husband died years ago. She took care of me; she bought land for me and built a house up the road from here. I missed being with her, so I started coming by here to spend time with her. She prepared a room for me in her home."

Thirteen

SHATTERED IMAGE
I THOUGHT I KNEW YOU,
BUT I GUESS I WAS WRONG

According to the elderly woman, Ebony learned that her mother had passed away in New York City. "She ordered the death certificate from that computer, you know how y'all young folks do. Anyway, she searched the Social Security death index and put her mother's name in it; that thing lets you put a first name or last name, and it will search city, state, or date of birth. She found her mother and learned she committed suicide. You know the people in New York took her children, and that child probably did not know what to do to get them back. So girls, Ebony did not have a mama. However, she was a mama to so many people. She got this big house to help children in foster care, and she gave so much money to people." Kenya said, "Excuse me, who is Ebony's business associate?" According to the elderly woman, that girl met Ebony about eight years ago. Ebony mentored her about business ownership. Ebony was part-owner of Pearl's business. However, Pearl did not have anything to do with Ebony's business.

Kenya asked the woman, "Why didn't she call you to tell you that Ebony died?" "I do not think that she had my numbers. Ebony was so private with her affairs. You young people do not take care of your business correctly, because you think that y'all gonna be here forever. You people keep everything in your telephones, God only knows what will happen if you lose your phone. Ebony should have prepared a list of friends and family to contact in case of emergency or death. She should have left it with the church so that when they got news that she died, that girl who conducts business with her would not be able to move so quickly. See, that girl probably gained something from Ebony's death. Ebony called me from the hospital and said the doctor told her she would be fine. However, she went in but never came out. She died of pneumonia. Her business associate said that Ebony had lupus or sarcoidosis. Yeah, those doctors could not tell what that child had. You know, a lot of y'all girls have those sicknesses. You do not attend the doctor regularly, and you do not eat or maintain a proper diet or exercise properly. Many of you are overworked and stressed. Everyone is looking for a big payout before going on vacation or something. Sometimes a walk in the park or quiet day alone or hot bath is what the doctor ordered.

Many of you wait until it is too late to get yourselves checked out. You can request or demand that a doctor take blood tests for lupus and other forms of illnesses, like sarcoidosis, as well as the CEA testing and CA-125 test for ovarian cancer. Your generation has more resources than when I was growing up to learn about diseases before they become fatal or end-stage. Through proper testing like urinalysis, chemical analysis, CBC, CEA test, ultrasounds, MRI, CAT scans and X-rays, you people can check for lung, ovarian and other cancers. Y'all have a lot more options than in my day. Some of you waste your money on foolishness, when you need to pay for your medical services. Some of you use that computer to research foolishness, when you should use it to learn about medical tests and things to save your life.

"The doctor told her years ago that she would probably not live to see 40 years of age. He was right. She has been ill ever since I have known her. She's been on medication. When she came back from Atlanta, she had changed a lot. She lost her will to fight. With all the material possessions that she had, she still felt empty. She does not have parents, family, a husband or children. She went to church regularly and loved the Lord the way she knew how, and she gave regularly to the community and people in need. She was tired of life all of a sudden, and I do not know why. Well, enough of that, what are you girls doing?" "Well, we wanted to say goodbye in our own way, but it was too late to go to the cemetery. Therefore, we went to sleep. Sahara had a vision that Ebony was at a safe in a room located in the basement. She saw her open it and saw the numbers and letters." "Oh, she does not have a basement here. The only place that I can think of that has a basement is the office building where I did the janitorial work, or my home, which is the house that she built." "Well, we think the basement may mean here on the main floor of this home," replied Mahogany. "Okay, suit yourself, but let me give you the keys to that office building and my place up the road. You cannot miss it; it is on the same land." Kenya asked, "How many acres is this property?" The woman replied, "It is about 81 acres. Ebony was a smart girl, because she bought land. You people go to the big city and buy those houses for all that money, pay on it for thirty years and never own anything. Sometimes you get it taken from you. I suggested that she purchase land. She owned a lot of land in different areas." "Did she ever mention a will?" asked Mahogany. "I reckon so, but I do not know where she kept it. It must be in that office building or something. Let me go with y'all, because I know the sheriff in this town, and he knows me. Someone sees y'all, and he or she will call the law." "Well, yeah, come on, because we do not need any problems," replied Sahara.

Upon arriving at the building, they searched the basement. They located a safe in the basement, but the basement did not have a room. Kenya attempted to open the safe using the numbers and letters in the vision, but to no avail. They tried using the numbers every way, but to no avail. Then Sahara said, "What year did Ebony's mother die?" The old woman told them the month, date, and year. Using those numbers and the letters from her mother's name, the safe opened. It was full of cash, insurance policies, business documents and other items of importance, but no will. They gathered those items and proceeded to go through her office to search. They never found any information.

Oddly enough, they found the name of her doctor and his telephone number. The old woman noticed that no one touched anything on Ebony's desk. Sahara asked her why that was important. She replied that it appeared that her business associate did not make a sincere attempt to locate them. Sahara asked her, "How do you know?" "Look right here, her Rolodex is in this drawer. All the business people in town have these. See, all of your numbers and emails are right here, and my personal information is listed here under 'M'," replied the old woman. "I thought you said that she had a separate business from Ebony?" "Correct. Pearl should have come over here to look herself, rather than funeralizing her without us," said the old woman. "There ought to be a law against that." Kenya said, "Ma'am, if a law existed, we would not be entitled to any more rights than Pearl." Crying, the old woman said, "Well, y'all known her all your life, and I've known her for more than 10 years, and I lived with her. Pearl just worked for her. Years ago, we gave the pastor of the church our will under seal, and some folks file them with the court or give copies to family and closest friends. Nowadays, everything is a big secret," said the old woman. "Besides, you cannot trust all pastors like yesteryear.

"Besides, y'all folks do not stay in touch as y'all should. A day should not end where no one calls to check on you. Y'all knew she was alone." Mahogany said, "No, ma'am, we thought she was here with her mother." The old woman asked, "Where did you get that foolishness?" Sahara replied, "That is what we thought and understood. We were wrong, because we made many assumptions. We thought that she was on a business trip or at a conference." The old woman asked, "Well, what do y'all use those cell phones for? It ain't no excuse that y'all did not stay in touch. I know that when the good Lord says that it is time to go home, it's time, and there ain't nothing no one can do," she exclaimed.

"Well, let us go check my basement, because I am curious. I have a room in my basement, and I do not think she would have any reason to keep a will there. Surely, she would outlive me, huh?" said the old woman. Upon arriving at the door, they immediately went to the basement. The basement had a room which had a closet that had the name RMR written across it. They entered the room and opened the closet. Behind the beautiful red velvet blanket was a safe. They tried her mother's information first, but to no avail. Then they tried the numbers and letters from the vision. The safe opened. Inside, there was money, insurance policies, signed and notarized deeds, photographs, birth certificates and death certificates, but no will. There was a letter in a separate envelope. They all sat in the basement and read the letter. It read:

> By now, I am sure that my old friend and my sisters Kenya, Sahara, and Mahogany are grieving my death. Grieve not, for I will forever be with you. Each of you remained with me until my death. I always knew that my life on this Earth would be short-lived. My memory, however, will live longer than I ever imagined. God orchestrated that, and I am content. I have suffered in silence for a long time, the only person who really heard my cry was my Lord and Savior Jesus Christ.

> What does it profit a man to gain the whole world and lose his soul? I lived by those words and aspired to give a gift of life to people who were in need. We all have different gifts of life. My gift was monetary. I tried to impart wisdom and knowledge as well. I acquired great wealth in this lifetime. My wealthiest gain was our meeting in Atlanta. What I gained carried me into Heaven. It prepared me for my travel home, my preparation home to face death. I finally achieved closure. I lived with hopes of finding my mother and siblings.

By now, you know that never happened. I lived for that very moment when my mother or sister would walk through my front door. I never realized that God gave me sisters when he gave me each of you. He gave me a mother when he blessed me with my old friend. I aspired for materialism in hopes that they would one day hear of me, or I could pay to find them anywhere in the world.

Why God chose this life for me to live is a question that I asked all of the time. However, I could not wait for an answer. I was tired, very tired. I wanted to leave this Earth. I could make this choice, and no one could take that away from me.

All of you are the beneficiaries to policies. Get a copy of the death certificate and file a claim. Divide equally amongst yourselves the money that is located inside the envelope. Four deeds are on file with the local court. I took care of that. Each of you has acquired the land. The office building is for a ministry for children and mothers in need. Use the other two policies to fund the programs. I have left instructions for someone else to handle all other matters. Finally, this property belongs to my old friend; she knows what to do with this home, my property, and the land. Yeah, I am sure that she has led you to believe that she does not know a lot about this. However, of all people, she does!

Ruth, Magdalene, and Rahab,

I want you to be blessed forever and encouraged by God. Hold on to the image in which He created.

Love Always,

Esther

Fourteen

BEYOND THE BOOK: Reader's Circle

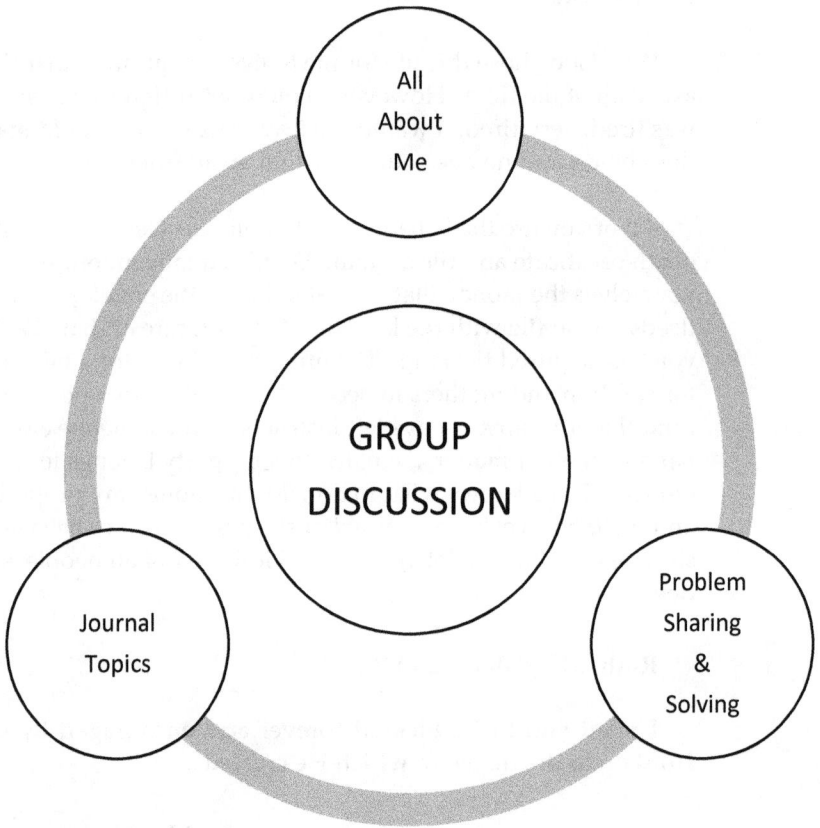

All
About
Me

GROUP
DISCUSSION

Journal
Topics

Problem
Sharing
&
Solving

ALL ABOUT ME

1. Discover who I am.
2. Rediscover who I am and what I am destined to be in this world.
3. Redefine, reorganize and reprioritize what is truly important to me.
4. Why am I "this" or "that" way?
5. Am I capable of changing and if so why or why not?
6. What must I do to better my own life.
7. Who owes me and why?
8. Life. What does it really mean?
9. My future. I see myself in 3-5 years (5-7, 7-10, 10-15 years) doing . . .
10. Am I content in my marriage (or singleness) and why. What must I do to change my circumstances for the better.
11. Am I better or bitter with my life and why?
12. Before I can become a friend to someone else, I must befriend myself. So how do I accomplish this goal?
13. A friend is . . .?
14. Why do I need friends in my life?
15. What are the benefits of this "friendship" and what do I bring to or I take away from the friendship?
16. What makes me unique?
17. Saved, but not delivered.
18. No do overs!

JOURNAL TOPICS

1. Why am I married (or single)?
2. My childhood dreams were, and I have (or have not) accomplished my goals. Why?
3. What must I do to reach . . .?
4. What steps must I take to better my life and those around me?
5. Am I my greatest obstacle and why?
6. My spouse means this to me . . .
7. My children mean this to me. . .
8. I am barren but not without child. . .
9. Being a wife means. . .
10. My employer means this to me…
11. I need a spouse, employer or… Why?
12. What is attention and how do I give it or receive it?
13. If I had 24 hours to live, I would…
14. My bucket list is….
15. My goal for the year is…
16. Failure means…
17. Success means…
18. Love is…
19. Hate is…
20. Destiny is…
21. Purpose is…
22. A calling is…
23. To be chosen means…
24. Death means…

GROUP DISCUSSION & PROBLEM SHARING AND PROBLEM SOLVING

1. Help your friend get to the next level
2. Help your friend discover who they are without being judgmental
3. Encourage your friend to engage in self-examination
4. When is judging **not** being judgmental?
5. Keeping it 'real' or '100' means?
6. Your friend's really has an addiction, now what?
7. Your friend's spouse is cheating on them, now what?
8. You saw your friend's spouse with a same-sex partner, now what?
9. When is friend's business your business?
10. AID/HIV
11. Homosexuality
12. Lack of character and integrity
13. Character flaws v. Flawed Character
14. Developing lasting friendships.
15. Your friend is not perfect and neither are you
16. Forgiving and forgetting. Knowing the difference.
17. Second chance or Fair Chance.
18. A Change or A Chance
19. "Saved," but not delivered.

About The Author

Sherri Jefferson is an author, independent book publisher, attorney, advocate, and lecturer. She is also the founder of the Family Law Center, African American Juvenile Justice Project, Jefferson Publishing, and the Law Mobile. Through #FemaleNOTFeemale, she advocates against child sexual exploitation and sex slavery, and the collateral consequences associated with criminalizing the acts of the victims of human trafficking and prostitution.

www.SherriJefferson.com